The
WRITE
HOUSE

Edwin Hurdle

Outskirts Press, Inc.
Denver, Colorado

Outskirts Press
http://www.outskirtspress.com

ISBN-10: 1-4327-0461-3
ISBN-13: 978-1-4327-0461-2

Outskirts Press and the "OP" logo are trademarks belonging to
Outskirts Press, Inc.

Printed in the United States of America

Introduction

There's a commander in writing. Pens and pencils are weapons where they don't cause any mass destruction. They fill the hands gracefully causing a flood of thoughts in our minds. A piece of paper is being used as a wall. A wall for beautiful words and deep feelings that are shared through the eyes and hearts of people. Poetry is a great form of literature ready to be written. There are poems about love, life, rejection, dreams and realities. The doors of my house are ready to be open where you are welcome to experience poetry at its truest form.

Contents

Dedication

This book is dedicated to Raymond Broadnax.

"A SON'S BEST FRIEND"

A man's best friend is his dog.
A woman's best friends are diamonds.
A son's best friend is his mother.
I am very proud to call my mother, my best friend.
She is the epicenter of my life.
I love her so much.
I thank her for giving me wings to fly.
I thank her for giving me glasses to see.
Without her, I would be nothing.
She never stabs me in the back.
Being there for me whenever I'm down so that I can get back up.
She tries so hard to raise this prince into a king.

Having her in my life is the greatest award.
I'm grateful to have such a beautiful and caring mother.
Every son should appreciate his mother's love.
Don't ever take it for granted.

"MY EQUAL"

She is my soulmate, my significant other, my rock, and my everything. She's the reason why God is blushing; as he witness this angel of beauty caressing the earth. There is a glow in the sky; the glow of her presence penetrating through the heavens. Her voice echoes in my dreams as the thought of her being a part of my life comes true. She's the reason why there is a storm along the seas, causing a tidal wave of love inside of me that is strong and intense. She's as sweet as any sugary substance which is why I'm diabetic for her love. She's the sun that sets in my heart and rise above in my spirits. I feel like Yankee player Lou Gerig: I am indeed the luckiest man on the face of this earth by having her be a part of my everyday existence.

"MVP"
(MOST VALUABLE PERSON)

She is the MVP of my life.
I am very proud to say.
Scoring points with love and
happiness.
Where she doesn't have to play.
She don't have to be athletic like
Micheal Jordan.
Or drive cars like Danica Patrick.
She doesn't have to sign a
contract to be with me.
My love for her is guaranteed
where there are no dirty tricks.
She doesn't have to win titles.
I will love her for being an
individual.
She doesn't have to take steroids.
My feelings for her are very spiritual.

She will always be the MVP of my life.
The number that she will always wear is #1 in my heart.
Words can't describe how I truly feel.
My love for her will never be broken apart.

"INGREDIENTS FOR ROMANCE"

2 hearts beating with unconditional love for one another.
A dozen candles being place all over the room.
A dozen love songs which put the mood into a fever's pitch.
Sweeping her off her feet like a broom.
2 cups of cuddles so that we can be close.
A lot of kisses to make it delicious.
An ounce of happiness to satisfy our feelings.
No cups of hatred will be allowed to make it vicious.
2 glasses are being set on the table.

Putting red wine in them, giving each other a toast.
Our eyes glitter to the fact that we are together.
Knowing that this recipe means the most.
We will always be hungry for romance.
That is what everybody is supposed to live by.
Being intimate is the key to it.
Loving each other until the day we die.

"HIGHER UPS, LOWER DOWNS"

This world has a corrupt
government.
They don't care about people of
color or the lower class.
Leaving us stranded with no end in
sight or no direction to go.
As if we were pieces of broken
glass.
Right now they are laughing at us
with their wicked grins.
They don't care whether we die or
live.
People of my race don't deserve
this kind of treatment.
Something's got to give.
The government treats us like
toilet paper.

They use all of us to wipe their backsides with.
Flushing each and every one of us down the toilet bowl.
Everything that happens to us is no myth.
It is a sad reality that we have already encountered.
I always ask myself the same question by saying why
We are not wild and sadistic animals.
We are hard-working human beings who deserve a piece of the American Pie.

"QUESTIONS WITHOUT ANSWERS"

Why do we have to die?
Do we go to heaven or hell?
Why does a cat have 9 lives?
What can you possibly tell?
Where are the angels?
Are there in the sky?
Why does the devil exist?
What makes people tell the truth
or lie?
What happens if there are no days
or time?
Is it possible that the world come
to a stand still?
How come water has to be clear?
Why can't non-famous people put
their faces on dollar bills?
When will the world be a peaceful

place to live?
When will racism end?
Why do people have to start
trouble?
Why can't we be friends?

"ME"

When I look in the mirror, whom do
I see?
ME
A 5'8 280 pound chocolate covered
Teddy Bear.
No gang colors to represent who I
am.
I don't have to take steroids to have
muscles.
Or have billions of dollars to be rich.
I may not be on the cover of GQ
magazine.
I am on the cover of ME
This is who I am.
I won't let anybody make me feel
less of a man or a human being.
Love me or hate me
Just accept ME!

"I USED TO LOVE YOU"

I used to love you.
Being there for you as a friend.
You are a criminal in my eyes.
By killing our friendship with a
knife so that it will end.
I used to love you.
My trust and kindness made you
feel strong.
You took it for granted all the time.
Going back to your jealous
boyfriend was wrong.
I used to love you.
On your birthday, I tried to say a
special greeting.
I felt like Rodney King from your
disrespectful words.
My heart took an enormous
beating.

I used to love you.
You are a distant memory.
My favorite subject in high school
was social studies.
I consider you history.

"A SPECIAL LADY"

I love you very much.
That is the honest truth.
I wouldn't trade you for anything.
The way the Red Sox trade Babe
Ruth.
My love for you is an addiction.
It will never go away where it leads
to a cure.
My feelings are not fake like
Micheal Jackson's nose.
They are passionate and pure.
Always remember that you are not
Hillary Swank.
You are the true million-dollar baby
in my life.
The love that I have is a weapon.
It penetrates through your body
like a sharp knife.

Ray Charles said it best; you are so beautiful to me.
I'm grateful to found someone as special as you are.
I don't have to be an astronaut in terms of going outer space.
You will always be my true shining star.

"Romance Avenue"

It is a special avenue that is located between the boulevard of intimacy and the street of love. A traffic light represents the love that I have for her, as it will always continue to go without ever stopping. The zip code is in the bedroom where I lift her up in my arms, being amazed by the creativity and charm that I truly possess, rose petals fills the room like a flood where tears of happiness rolls down the side of her face; witnessing how much she has mean to me. Thousands and thousands of candles spelling out I love you as I serenade her with my poetic words, where I hold her hand and look deep into her eyes which is the window to her soul. The romantic prowess that I have makes this avenue very special.

"WHAT IT FEELS LIKE TO BE A VICTIM"

I was a victim of a robbery several
years ago.
Being robbed of my gold chain.
He had a small knife in his hand.
Not knowing whether he will cause
me pain.
My body was numb.
My heart was beating fast.
If I didn't give him what he wanted.
My time on this earth may not
have last.
On the same day, the cops
arrested the perpetrator.
I didn't get the gold chain back.
He sold it to someone.
For some drugs like crack.
As long as I live, I will never forget

what happen.
Thinking about it every single day.
That bastard belongs in jail where
he belongs.
Realizing that crime doesn't pay.

"DIFFERENT COLORS SAME TASTE"

The world is like a big box of ice cream.
It consists of flavors to satisfy anyone's taste.
Each of them is sweet and special.
They should not go to waste.
My heart is a bowl fill with acceptance.
Loving each flavor that comes in it.
If you combine all of them into one,
You'll get a rainbow of the human spirit.
Chocolate is the flavor that I'm proud of.
No need to put sprinkles or whip cream on me.

Everyone is supposed to love one
another without hatred.
The way that it is meant to be.
At the end of the day, we are all
flavors of unity.
One should not discriminate over
the other.
In the mirror we see the same
reflection.
As being true sisters and brothers.

"JUST BECAUSE"

Just because I'm not a tough guy doesn't mean that I'm less of a man.
I don't have to prove my masculinity to anyone by doing those things.
The fact that I'm authentic makes me more of a man.
I'm not going to let anybody turn me into a puppet where they control all the strings.
Just because I don't have a girlfriend doesn't mean that I'm lonely.
I'm exploring my options so that I will end up with Ms.Right instead of Ms.Wrong.
I'm everything that a woman wants in a man and then some.

Before you know it, I won't be single for any long.

Just because I don't have a lot of money doesn't mean that I'm poor.

I'm very rich due to how I appreciate the littlest things that matter.

Why should I have to be jealous of certain valuables that I don't possess?

I will climb higher to achieve goals without anybody pushing me off the ladder.

Just because I'm not sexy doesn't mean that I'm ugly.

My trillion-dollar smile and how I treat people makes me attractive.

I have a handsome, young face that any woman can love.

Where I don't have to get surgery or use proactive.

"PASSWORD TO A GOOD RELATIONSHIP"

A password is a combination of letters and numbers so that you can get online. There is a password to having a good relationship. It doesn't require any numbers. It is a 4-letter word that is very important. Love is the password that makes the relationship work. No one can ever take it away from you. Certain things in life maybe gone like money, house, or a job. Love will always stay forever. Love is what makes the relationship build stronger and stronger with each passing day.

"EVERYDAY SHOULD BE A HOLIDAY"

Treat each day as if it was special. Holidays shouldn't occur once a year. Everyday should be like Christmas. Give out presents to someone that you care about or do something nice for a stranger. Everyday should be like Valentine's Day. Showing unconditional love to your soul mate through the good and bad times. Everyday should be like a birthday. Enjoy your years as you grow with maturity. Everyday should be like Mother's or Father's Day. Children should appreciate what their parents have meant to them in their lives. Everyday should be like Thanksgiving. Family gatherings should take place several times a year. Don't take everyday for granted. Treat each day like a holiday fill with happiness without any regrets.

"SEL-FISH"

There are a lot of fishes that I've eaten from codfish to flying fish, but I will never try out this fish. It stinks so bad that it can lead to self-destruction. Hurting everybody in its path without any remorse or compassion. It is no good for anybody. There are plenty of fishes in the sea. I don't want to see this type of fish conquer the seas in our hearts where we are mean spirited toward one another. Don't ever try to catch it. Stay away from it as far as possible.

"MY FAVORITE CLASSROOM"

Life is a big classroom. Sometimes you pass and sometimes you fail. You meet interesting people and learn different things everyday to improve your life. You graduate when you grow up more and become a better person. There are many discoveries surrounding us that we are eager to know about. Giving a grade to everything we see, hear and experience. People shouldn't take life for granted. One day all of us will leave this world to meet the greatest teacher of them all.

"MY OWN WORLD"

When I go to the park, I'm at peace within myself. I don't have to hear people arguing over stupid things or hear cars honking as if they were a part of an orchestra. Getting away from the drama of the city where I come to a place that is refreshing. A beautiful waterfront park where I can view the city skyline. The cool breeze hugs my body as the smell of grass tickle my nose, appreciating the gift that Mother Nature has created where the spirit inside of me is release. The brightness from the sky comes from the children who are bless to enjoy the warm weather by their giggles and joyful screams. People walking their dogs with a sense of calm and happiness. Couples holding hands and kissing each other to express there true love. I am indeed a very lucky man to experience this special place. A different side of the world. My Own World

"BEING AN INDIVIDUAL"

It is something that I'm proud of. I don't have to be another human being or follow anybody's methods. All that I am is myself. I have my own mind where I can think whatever I want; I have my own mouth where I can speak the truth with powerful words. I have my own style that is ordinary and unique. Being myself is better than anything else in this world. It is better than any lifestyle that I live or any materialistic thing that I have. When I wake up and look in the mirror, I see an individual. A strong-minded individual with no fears of what people think about me. This is who I am; from the way

I look to the way that I conduct myself in front of people.120% all real all the time.

"6191982"

These numbers doesn't represent my weight or my phone number or the number to my address. It is not how many times that I got married or how many women that I've slept with. They don't represent my salary or how many times that President Bush was wrong about weapons of mass destruction in Iraq. These numbers represent who I am as they represent the time, day, and year that I was put here on this earth. I am blessed to be alive and I'm proud that these numbers symbolizes who I am as a human being.

"A PERFECT GENTLEMAN"

I'm the perfect gentleman who has
a heart of gold.
Treating women with the utmost
respect.
Holding doors for them or saying
ladies first.
Drawn to my kindness that they
didn't expect.
If a lady drops something, I will
pick it up.
She will show appreciation by
being thankful.
One time I brought a woman a cup
of hot chocolate.
I told her she looks absolutely
beautiful.
Nice guys don't always finish last.
Being a gentleman will always be

first on my agenda.
I will continue to treat women with
the greatest admiration.
No matter if your name is
Shaniqua or Melinda.
I will never abuse or disrespect
women by calling them names.
That is not how I was raised.
A woman likes a man who can
make them feel more important.
Having characteristics of a perfect
gentleman is what they will praise.

"THE GREATEST SOUND"

Shhhhh, don't make a sound.
Did you hear that?
Quiet is the sound that you hear.
No screams, just utter silence.
No gunshots firing, no people
arguing.
When things are quiet, it is
peaceful.
Quiet is your ears' best friend.
A tool that can fix any loud
disturbance.
It creates an environment where
people can concentrate.
Doing yoga with your mind as your
thoughts stretch deeply
Shhhhh, don't make any noise.
Quiet time is upon us

Printed in the United States
200285BV00008B/1-6/A